Etude Supplement For The Shape Method for Jazz Improvisation Vol. 2

Malcolm Lynn Baker

"I think that the idea that jazz can be learned by using a harmonic approach, as opposed to a melodic approach, is essentially a flawed philosophy. It's much easier to teach people the harmonic constructs than to force them to learn music by ear, which is far more difficult. One of the problems I have with a lot of today's jazz is the lack of melody and overemphasis on harmonic associations."

Branford Marsalis
Branford Marsalis Frankly Speaking
Marc Chenard, May 30, 2007.
http://www.scena.org/lsm/sm12-8/
sm12-8_marsalis_en.html

Cover art *Socks* by Kalin Baker. © 2014, www.kalinartandspirit.com

Copyright © 2014 by Malcor Music Publishing

All rights reserved. Printed in the United States of America. This publication is protected by Copyright and permission should be obtained from the publisher prior to any prohibited reproduction, storage in a retrieval system, or transmission in any form or by any means, electronic mechanical, photocopying, recording, or likewise. To obtain permissions(s) to use material from this work, please submit a written request to Malcor Music Publishing, 4485 @ 61st Place, Arvada, CO 80003.

Table of Contents

Introduction to *The Etude Supplement for The Shape Method* i

1. Anchor Phrases (TSM, Ch. 8) 1
2. Neighbor Tones (TSM, Ch. 9) 8
3. Micro-Resolutions with Triplets, Ascending (TSM, Ch. 11) 16
4. Micro-Resolutions with Triplets, Descending (TSM, Ch. 11) 23
5. Micro-Resolutions with Sixteenths (TSM, Ch. 14) 30
6. Extended Bi-Directional Resolutions (TSM, Ch. 14) 36
7. Super-Impositions on Minor and Major Triads (TSM, Ch. 16) 52
8. Super-Impositions on Dominant Chords I (TSM, Ch. 17) 54
9. Dominant Chords II (TSM, Ch. 18) 60
10. Quartal Materials (TSM, Ch. 21) 62
11. Four Tonic System (TSM, Ch. 22) 65
12. Three and Six Tonic Systems (TSM, Ch. 23) 70

Etude Supplement for
The Shape Method for Jazz Improvisation
Lynn Baker

INTRODUCTION

The Shape Method is focused on ways to develop excellent jazz solos through concepts of melodic and rhythmic shape. The text provides rhythmic and phrase-shape concepts derived from bebop solo practice of many master improvisers, and at the conclusion of each chapter provides composition and performance assignments. The performance assignments are stated in a generalized way and the student is invited to create their own etudes based on the materials. Students are still encouraged to do this, but *Etude Supplement, Vol. 1 and Vol. 2* provide further guidance for developing the improvisation techniques of *The Shape Method*.

Vol. 1 contains etudes that focus on diatonic and chromatic approaches to Consonance Tones of Major and Minor triads. *Vol. 2* contains more extended harmonies and ideas that provide further chromatic colors.

CONVENTIONS

Standard jazz chord notation is used throughout. All meters are 4/4. Due to the nature of these concepts there is a lot of chromaticism in the etudes; every attempt was made to not mix flats and sharps, but sometimes that was necessary. In addition, F Flat and C Flat are uncommon notes to read and are most useful in theoretical analysis and not performance, therefore sometimes enharmonic intervals result – get over it.

HOW THE SUPPLEMENT IS ORGANIZED

The *Etude Supplement* is coordinated with the phrase-shape concepts discussed in *The Shape Method*. The Table of Contents contains notations regarding which chapters of *The Shape Method* are being addressed. Multi-page etudes begin on even pages to facilitate performing all the keys without turning pages and allowing transposing instruments to play the etudes together.

The Shape Method - Introduction

HOW TO USE THE SUPPLEMENT

Here are suggested ways to use the *Etude Supplement*:

1) Play all etudes in all keys along with *The Shape Method* chapter in which they were assigned:

    a. For etudes that are specifically key oriented, play them a variety of key relationships:

        i. In the circle of fifths, as they are presented in the text
        ii. In Ascending and/or Descending Minor 2nd relationships
        iii. In Ascending and/or Descending Major 2nd relationships
        iv. In Ascending and/or Descending Minor 3rd relationships
        v. In Ascending and/or Descending Major 3rd relationships
        vi. In Ascending and/or Descending Tri-tone relationships

    b. Etudes that are chromatic can be started at various places and "looped" to cover the entire area.

2) Play similar concepts (e.g., various forms of Bi-Directional Resolutions) in one key, then play all in another key, etc.

3) Play through the text in any order you'd like.

4) Play etudes in the key areas of pieces you are studying.

Etude Supplement, Vol. 2 – Chapter 1

Anchor Phrase #1

Anchor Phrase #2

Etude Supplement, Vol. 2 – Chapter 1

ANCHOR PHRASE #4

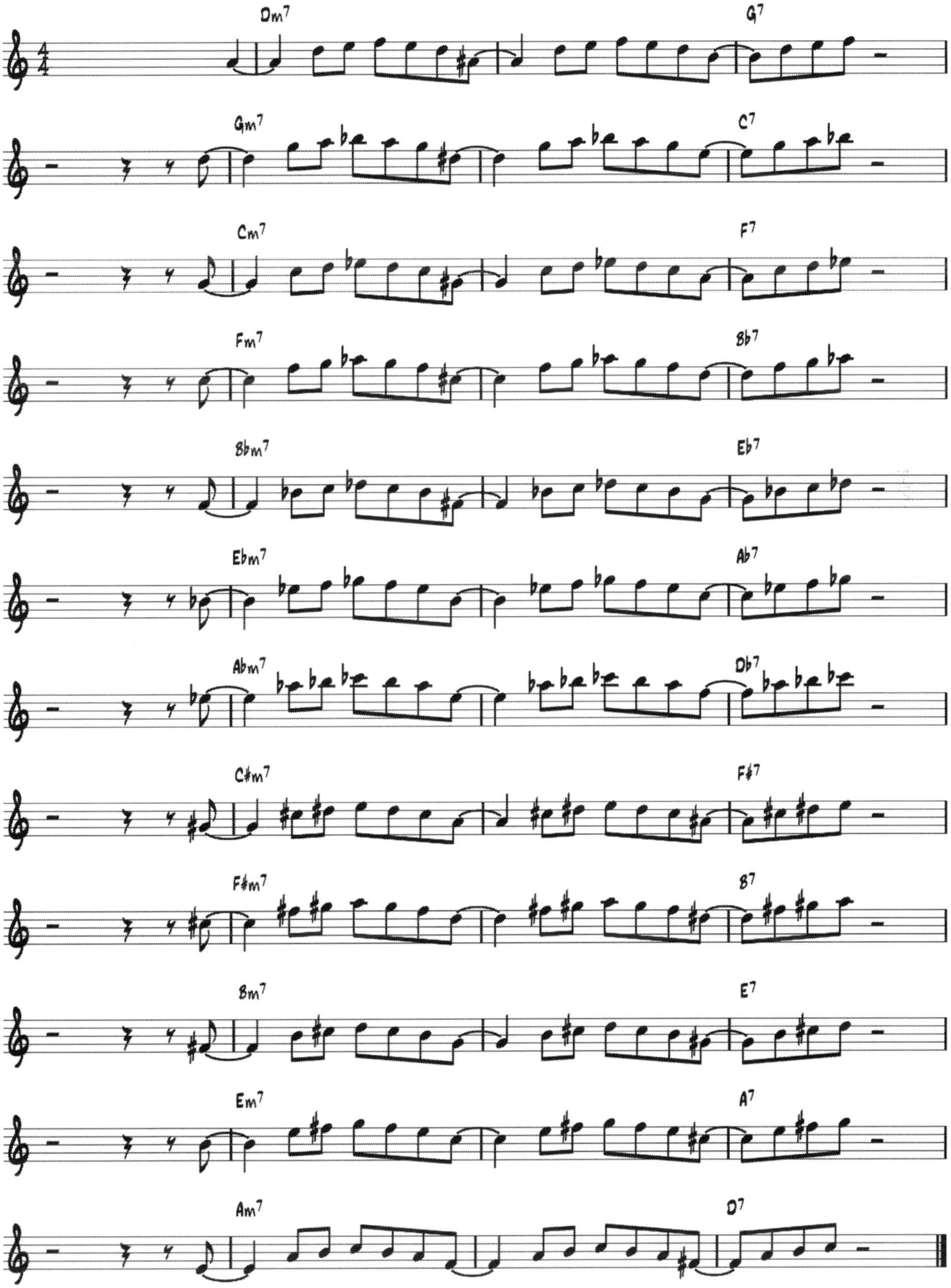

Etude Supplement, Vol. 2 – Chapter 1

Anchor Phrase #5

Etude Supplement, Vol. 2 – Chapter 1

Anchor Phrase #6

Anchor Phrase #7

Etude Supplement, Vol. 2 – Chapter 1

Anchor Phrase #10

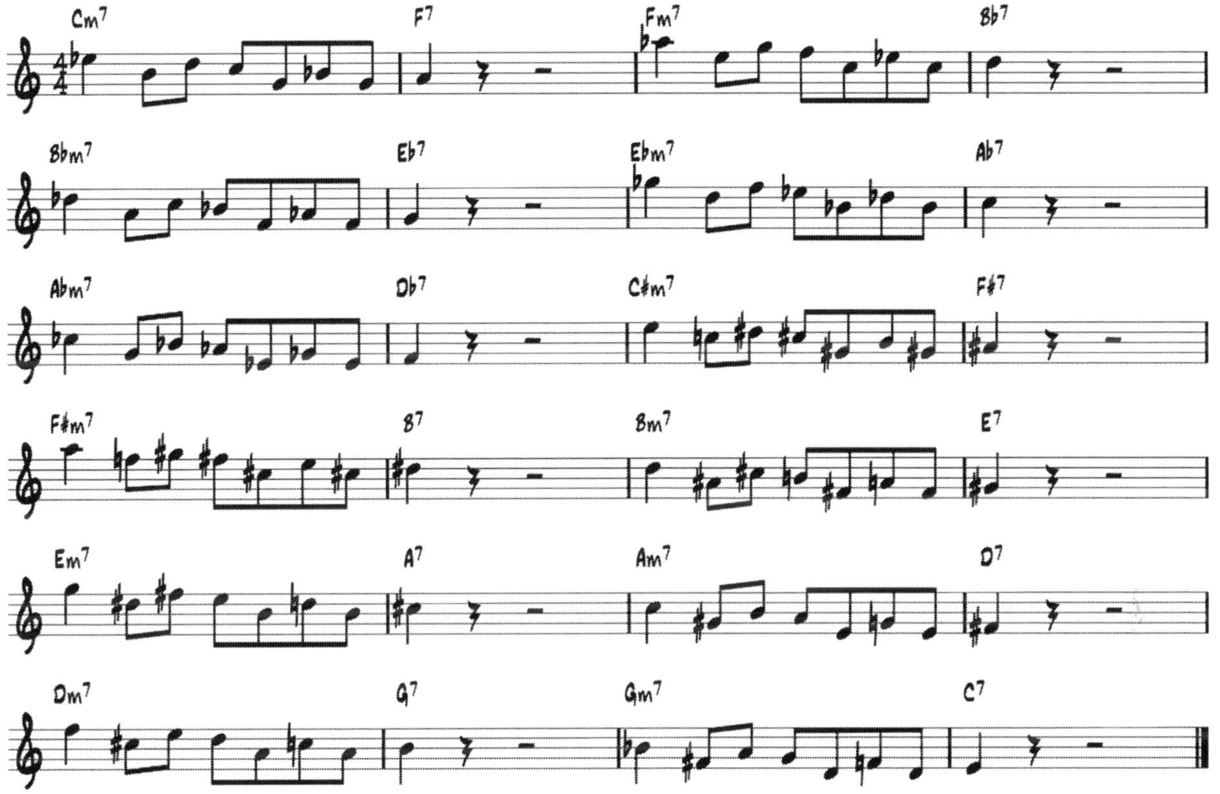

Etude Supplement, Vol. 2 – Chapter 2

Major Lower & Upper Diatonic Neighbor Tones

Etude Supplement, Vol. 2 – Chapter 2

Etude Supplement, Vol. 2 – Chapter 2

Minor Lower and Upper Diatonic Neighbor Tones

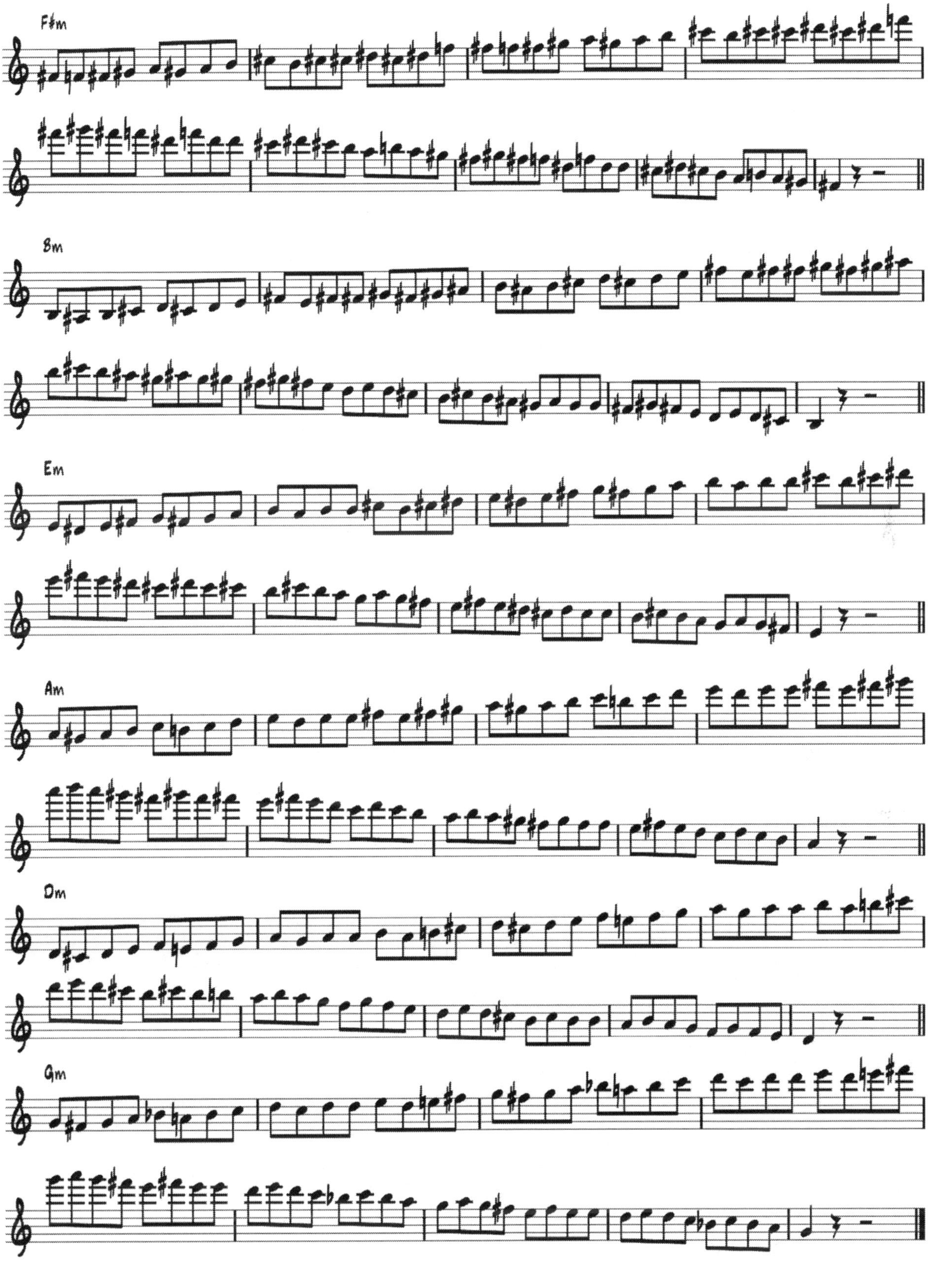
F#m
Bm
Em
Am
Dm
Gm

Etude Supplement, Vol. 2 – Chapter 2

Major Lower & Upper Chromatic Neighbor Tones

Etude Supplement, Vol. 2 – Chapter 2

Etude Supplement, Vol. 2 – Chapter 2

Minor Lower and Upper Chromatic Neighbor Tones

Etude Supplement, Vol. 2 – Chapter 2

Etude Supplement, Vol. 2 – Chapter 3

Maj 3 Triplets, Asc. by Half Steps, Beg. w/ Half Step

Maj 3 Triplets, Asc. by Half Steps, Beg. w/ Whole Step

Etude Supplement, Vol. 2 – Chapter 3

Maj 3 Triplets Ascending in M2nds, Beg. w/ Half Step

Maj 3 Triplets, Ascending by M2nds, Beg. w/ Whole Step

Etude Supplement, Vol. 2 – Chapter 3

Maj 3 Triplets, Asc. by M3rds, Beg. w/ Half Step

Maj 3 Triplet, Asc. in M3rds, Beg. w/ Whole Step

Maj 3 Triplets, Ascending by M3rds, Beg. w/ Half Step

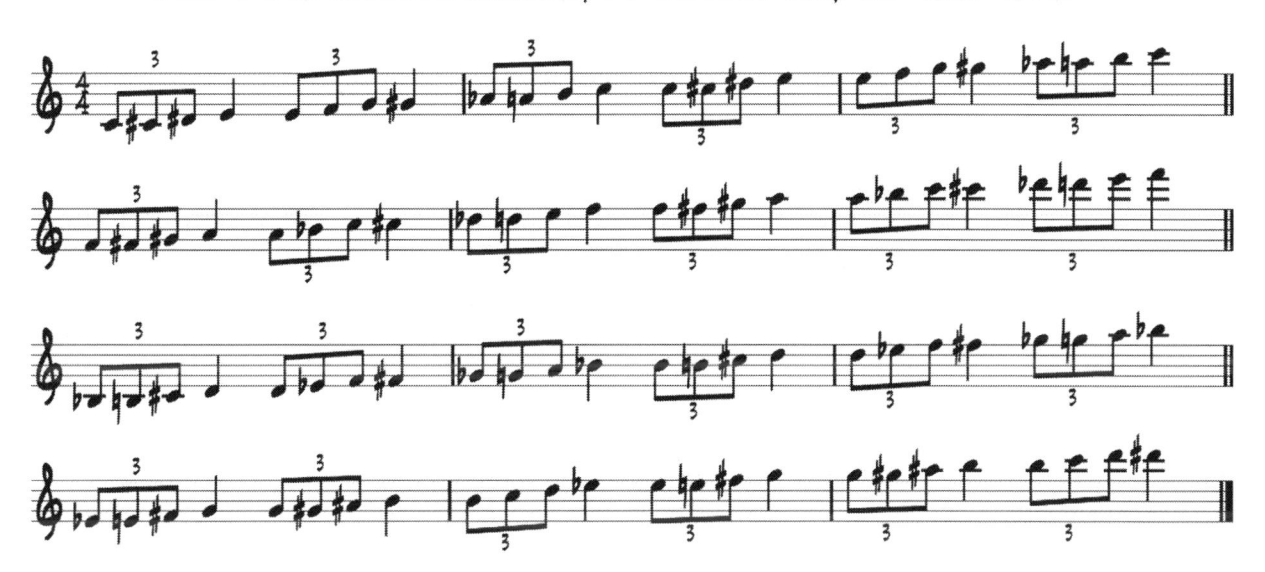

Maj 3 Triplets, Asc. by M3rds, Beg. w/ Whole Step

Maj 3 Ascending Triplets in 4ths, Beg. w/ Half Step

Maj 3 Triplets Ascending in 4ths, Beg. w/ Whole Step

Min 3rd Triplets, Asc. by M2nds

Min 3rd Triplets, Asc. by M2nds

Min 3rd Triplets, Asc. by M3rds

Min 3rd Tripets, Asc. by M3rds

Min 3rd Triplets asc. by 4ths

Etude Supplement, Vol. 2 – Chapter 4

Maj 3 Desc., Beg. w/ Half Step, Asc. by Min 2

Maj 3 Desc., Beg. w/ Whole Step, Asc. by Min 2

Maj 3 Desc., Beg. w/ Half Step, Asc. in Maj 2nds

Maj 3 Desc. Triplet, Asc. by Whole step, Beg. w/ Whole Step

Maj 3 Desc. Beg. w/ Half Step, Asc. by Min 3rds

Maj 3 Desc., Beg. w/ Whole step, Asc. by Min 3rds

Maj 3 Desc., Asc. by Maj 3, Beg. w/ Half-Step

Maj 3 Triplets, Asc. in Maj 3rds, Beg. w/ Whole Step

Maj 3 Desc. Triplets, Beg. w/ Half Step, in 4ths

Maj 3 Triplets Desc., Beg. w/ Whole Step, in 4ths

Etude Supplement, Vol. 2 – Chapter 4

MIN 3RD TRIPLETS DESC., ASC. IN M2NDS

MIN 3RD TRIPLETS DESC. IN ASC. M2NDS

Min 3rd Triplets Desc., Asc. in M3rds

Min 3rd Triplets Desc., Asc. in M3rds

Min 3rd Triplet Desc. in 4ths

Etude Supplement, Vol. 2 – Chapter 5

Maj 3 Descending Sixteenth in M2nds

Maj 3 Ascending Sixteenth in M2nds

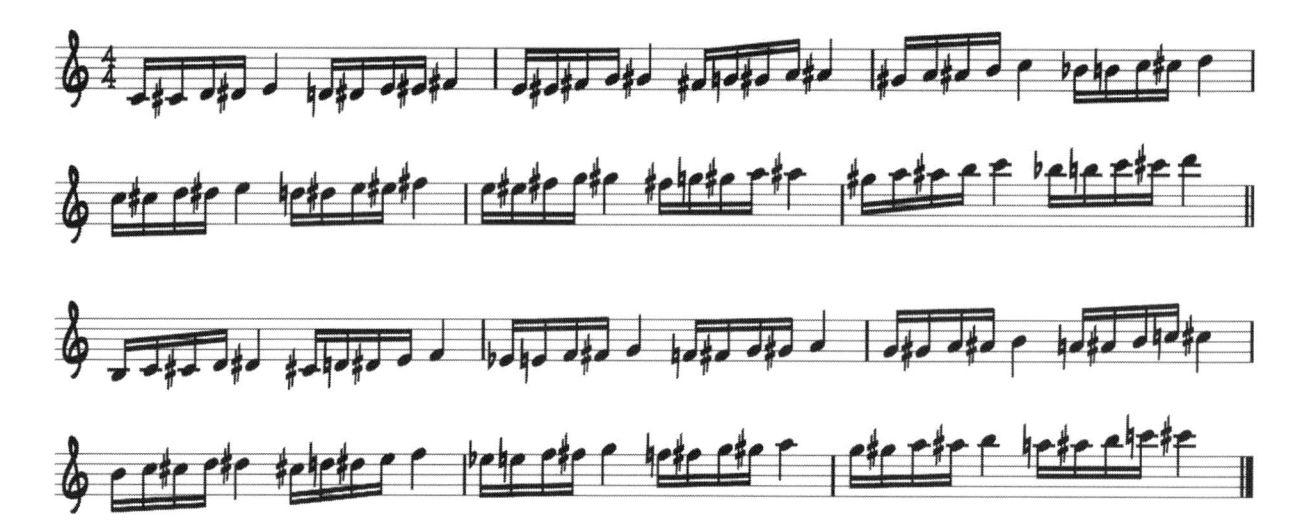

Maj 3 Ascending Sixteenth in M3rds

C, E Flat, F Sharp, & A

C Sharp, E, G, & B Flat

D, F, A Flat, & B

Maj 3 Ascending Sixteenth in M3rds

C, E, & G Sharp

C Sharp, F, & A

D, F Sharp, & B Flat

E Flat, G, & B

Maj 3 Ascending Sixteenth in 4ths

Maj 3 Ascending Sixteenth in M2nds

Maj 3 Ascending Sixteenth in M2nds

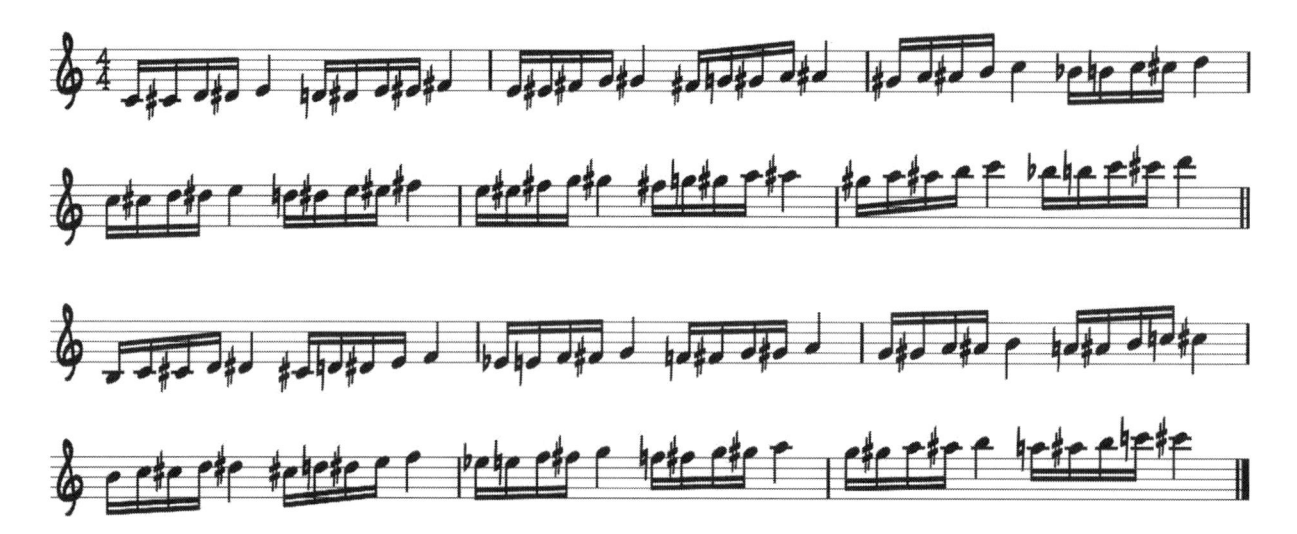

Maj 3 Ascending Sixteenth in M3rds

C, E Flat, F Sharp, & A

C Sharp, E, G, & B Flat

D, F, A Flat, & B

Maj 3 Ascending Sixteenth in M3rds

C, E, & G Sharp

C Sharp, F, & A

D, F Sharp, & B Flat

E Flat, G, & B

MAJ 3 ASCENDING SIXTEENTH IN 4THS

Etude Supplement, Vol. 2 – Chapter 6

Extended Major Bi-Directional Resolutions from Below, Nearest

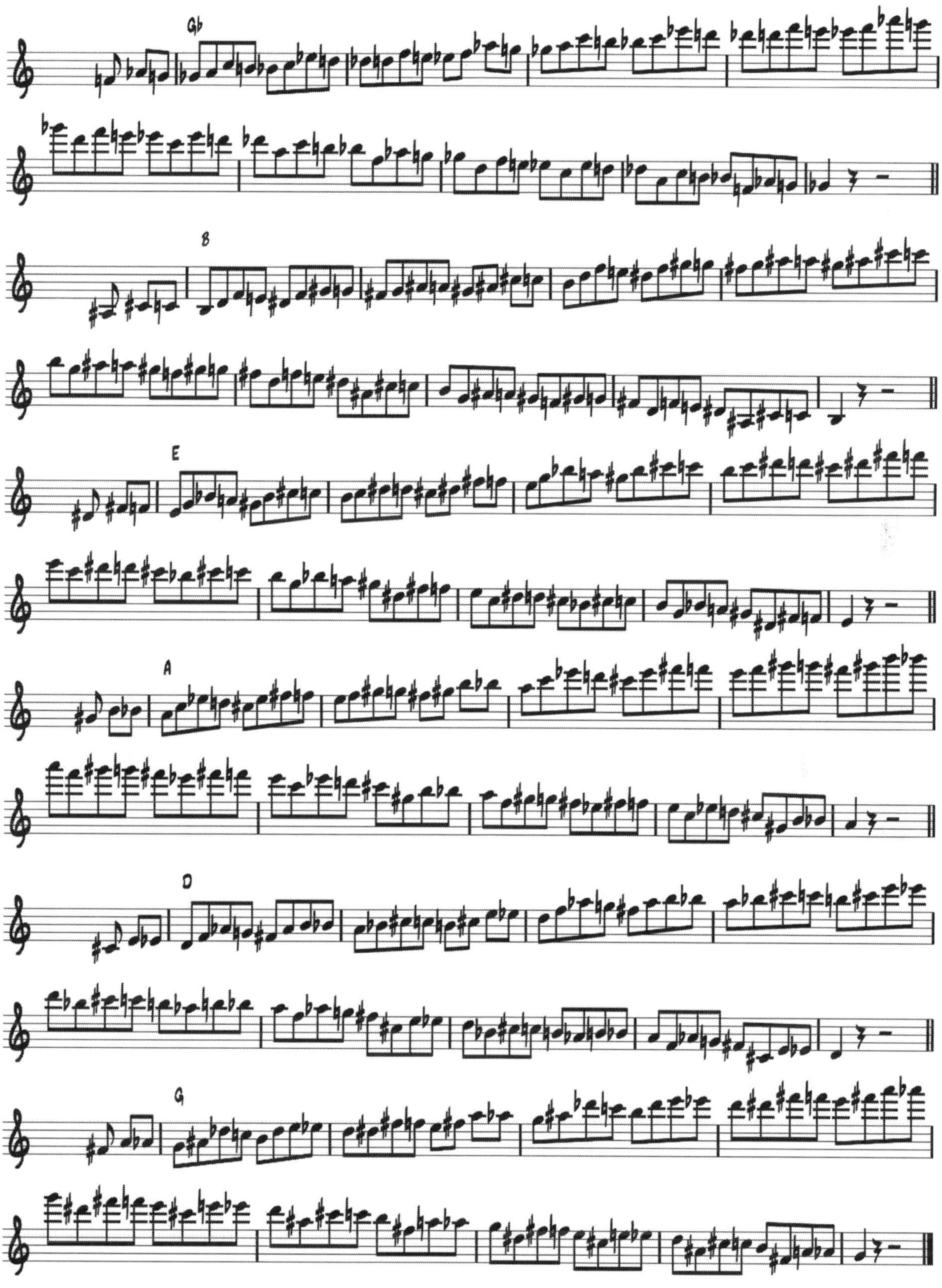
Gb
B
E
A
D
G

Etude Supplement, Vol. 2 – Chapter 6

EXTENDED MAJOR BI-DIRECTIONAL RESOLUTIONS FROM BELOW, FURTHEST

Etude Supplement, Vol. 2 – Chapter 6

Etude Supplement, Vol. 2 – Chapter 6

EXTENDED MAJOR BI-DIRECTIONAL RESOLUTIONS FROM ABOVE, NEAREST

Etude Supplement, Vol. 2 – Chapter 6

Extended Major Bi-Directional Resolutions from Above, Furthest

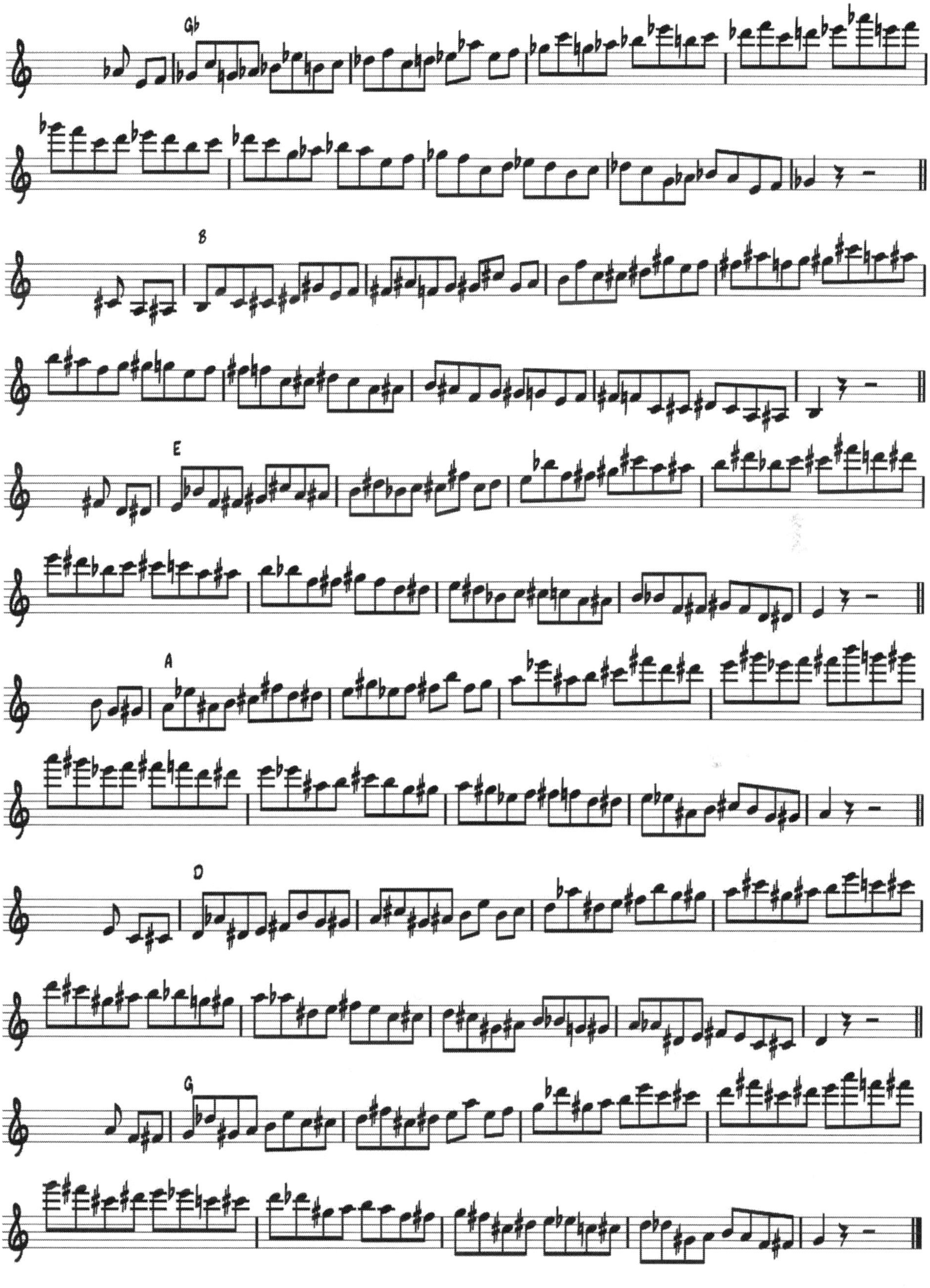
G♭
B
E
A
D
G

Etude Supplement, Vol. 2 – Chapter 6

EXTENDED MINOR BI-DIRECTIONAL RESOLUTIONS FROM BELOW, NEAREST

Etude Supplement, Vol. 2 – Chapter 6

Etude Supplement, Vol. 2 – Chapter 6

EXTENDED MINOR BI-DIRECTIONAL RESOLUTIONS FROM BELOW, FURTHEST

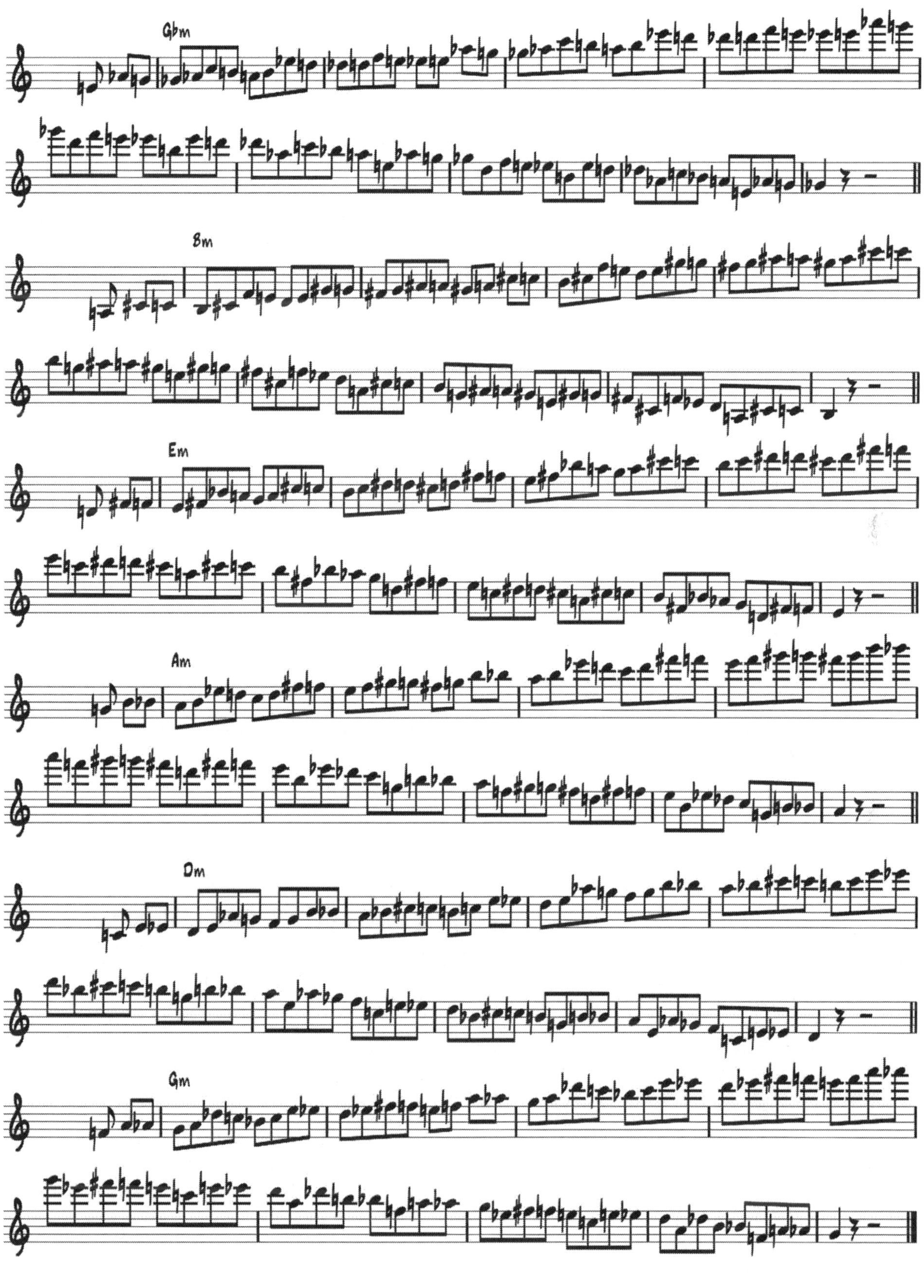
Gbm
Bm
Em
Am
Dm
Gm

Etude Supplement, Vol. 2 – Chapter 6

EXTENDED MINOR BI-DIRECTIONAL RESOLUTIONS FROM ABOVE, NEAREST

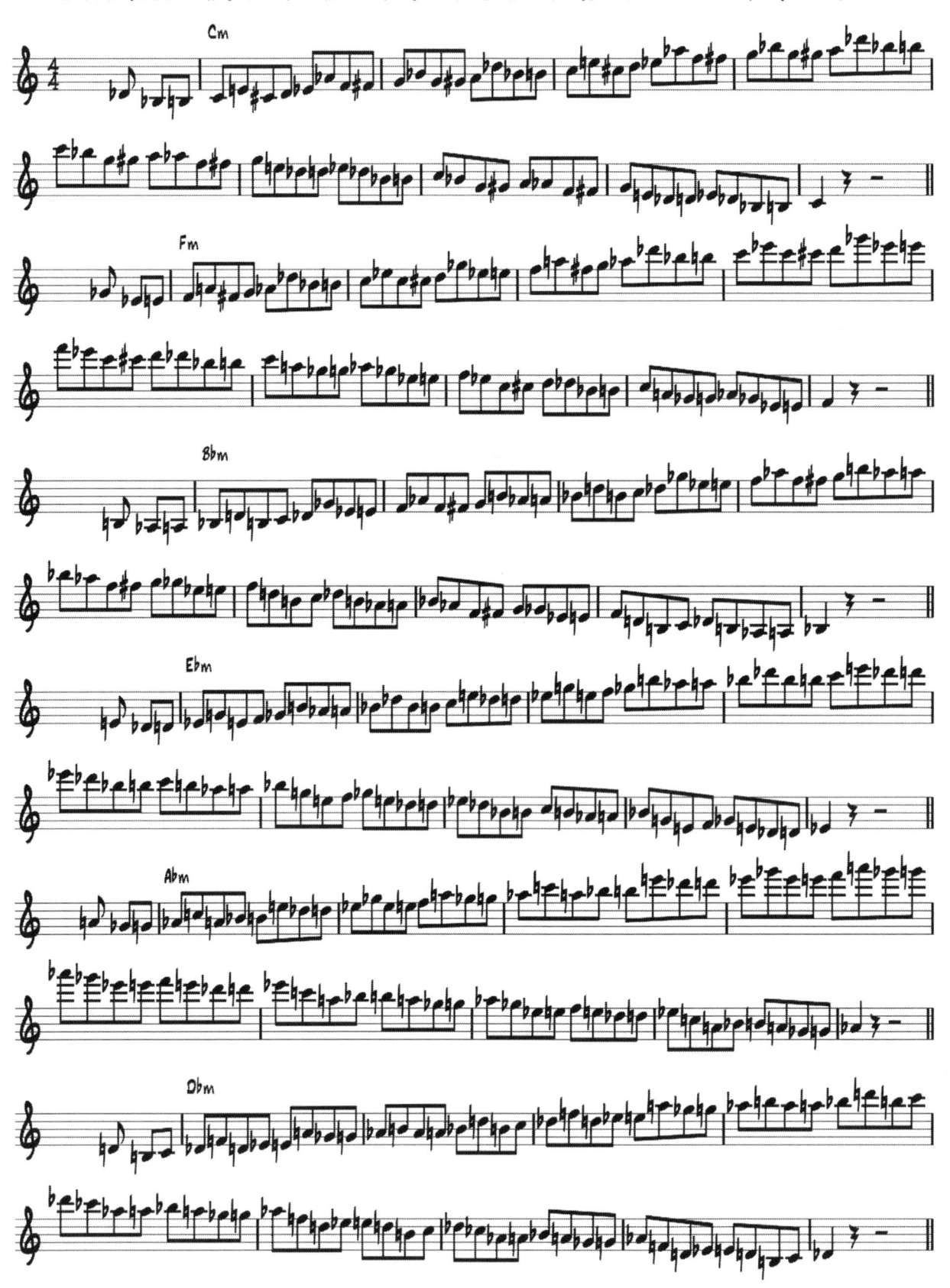

Etude Supplement, Vol. 2 – Chapter 6

Etude Supplement, Vol. 2 – Chapter 6

EXTENDED MINOR BI-DIRECTIONAL RESOLUTIONS FROM ABOVE, FURTHEST

Etude Supplement, Vol. 2 – Chapter 6

Minor with Flat VII Major Sup-Imp

Minor with Flat III Major Sup-Imp

Etude Supplement, Vol. 2 – Chapter 7

Major with Major II Sup-Imp

Major with III Minor Sup-Imp

Etude Supplement, Vol. 2 – Chapter 8

MAJOR WITH MAJOR II SUP-IMP

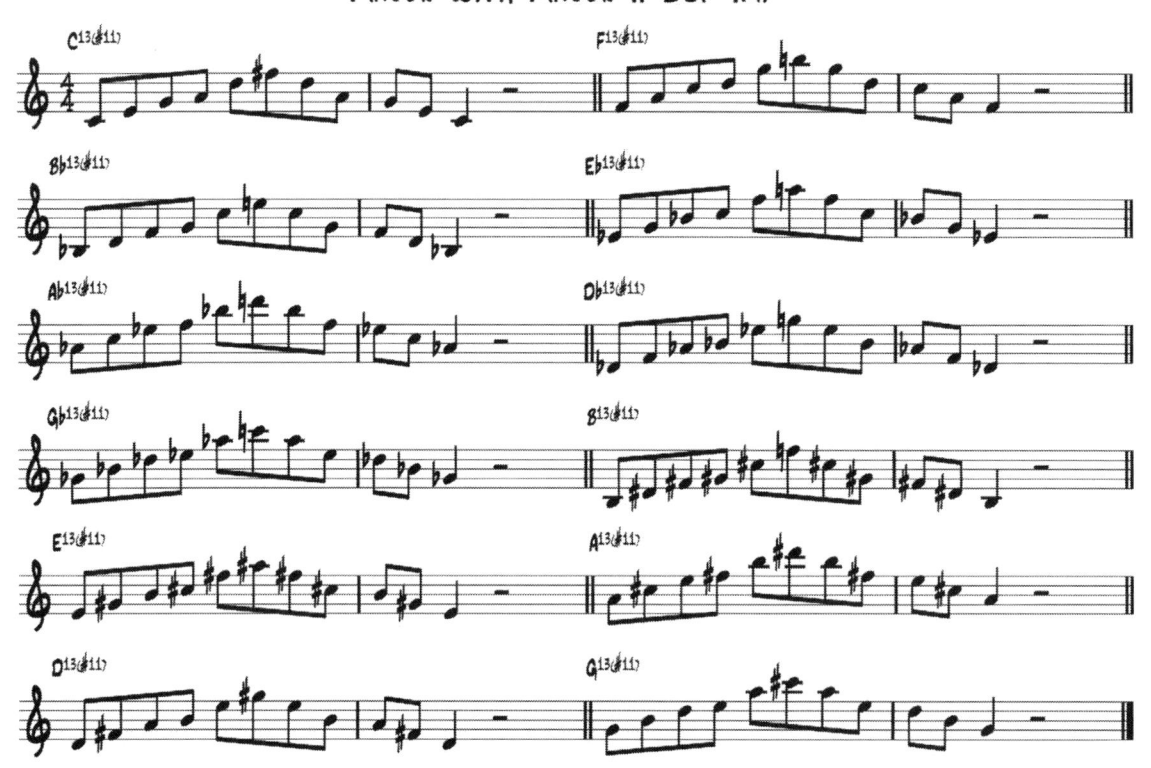

MAJOR WITH MINOR II SUP-IMP

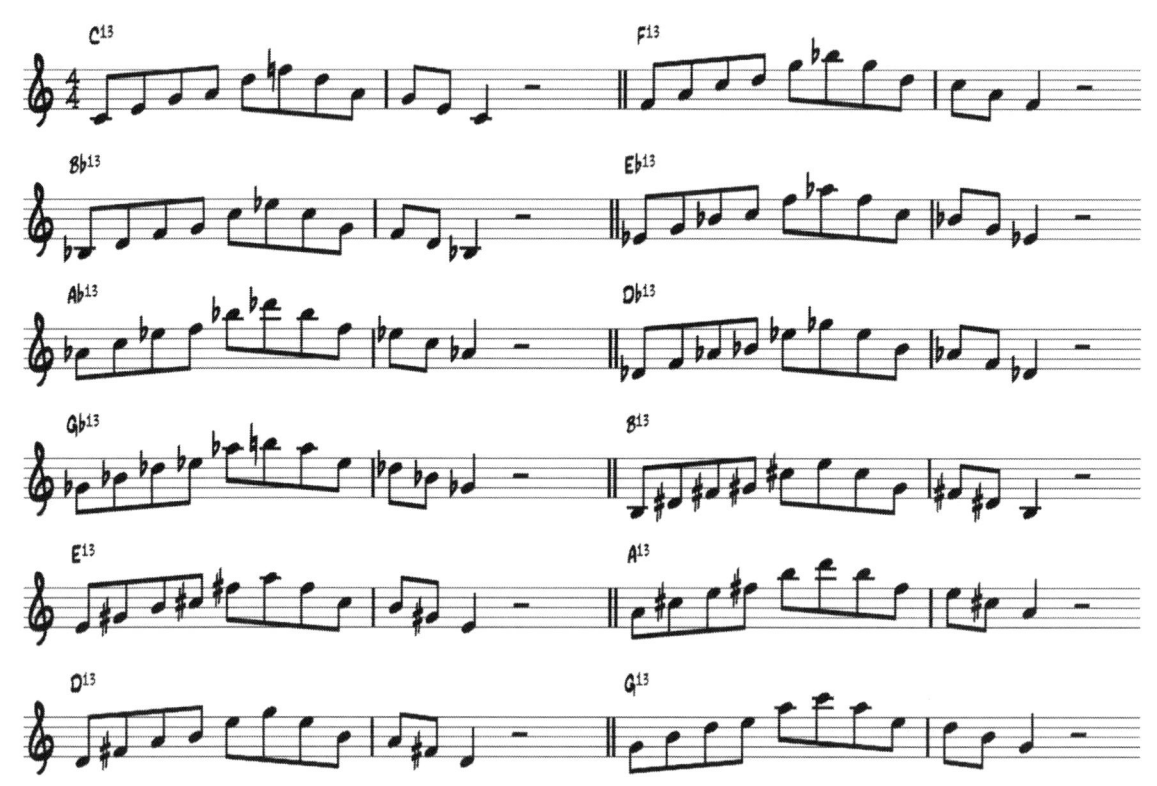

Etude Supplement, Vol. 2 – Chapter 8

Major with Flat III Major Sup-Imp

Major with Flat III Minor Sup-Imp

Etude Supplement, Vol. 2 – Chapter 8

Major with IV Major Sup-Imp

Major with #IV Major Sup-Imp

Major with #IV Minor Sup-Imp

Etude Supplement, Vol. 2 – Chapter 8

Major with Flat VII Major Sup-Imp

Major with Flat VII Minor Sup-Imp

Etude Supplement, Vol. 2 – Chapter 9

Major with Flat II Major Sup-Imp

Major with Flat II Minor Sup-Imp

Major with IV Minor Sup-Imp

Major with Flat VI Major Sup-Imp

Etude Supplement, Vol. 2 – Chapter 10

Minor with Flat VII Major Sup-Imp

Minor with Flat II Major Sup-Imp

Major with Flat II Minor Sup-Imp

Minor with IV Minor Sup-Imp

Etude Supplement, Vol. 2 – Chapter 10

Major Triad with Major V, II, or Minor II Sup-Imp

Etude Supplement, Vol. 2 – Chapter 11

Four Tonic Major Triads, Ascending

Four Tonic System Major Triads, Descending

Etude Supplement, Vol. 2 – Chapter 11

Four Tonic System, Major Triads Alt. Asc & Desc.

B Flat, D Flat, E, & G

B, D, F, & A Flat

C, E Flat, G Flat, & A

Four Tonic System, Major Traids Alt. Desc. and Asc.

B Flat, D Flat, E, & G

B, D, F, & A Flat

C, E Flat, G Flat, & A

Etude Supplement, Vol. 2 – Chapter 11

Four Tonic System, Minor Triads Ascending

Four Tonic System, Minor Triads Descending

Etude Supplement, Vol. 2 – Chapter 11

Four Tonic System, Minor Triads Descending

Four Tonic System, Minor Triads, Alt. Asc. & Desc.

B Flat, C Sharp, E, & G

B, D, F, & G Sharp

C, E Flat, F Sharp, & A

Four Tonic System, Minor Triads Alt. Desc. & Asc.

B Flat, C Sharp, E, & G

B, D, F, & G Sharp

C, E Flat, F Sharp, & A

Etude Supplement, Vol. 2 – Chapter 12

Etude Supplement, Vol. 2 – Chapter 12

Three Tonic Alt. Asc. and Desc.

Three Tonic Alt. Desc. and Asc.

Etude Supplement, Vol. 2 – Chapter 12

Three Tonic Line #1

Three Tonic Line #2

Etude Supplement, Vol. 2 – Chapter 12

Six Tonic Major Triads, All Asc.

Six Tonic Major Triads, All Desc.

Etude Supplement, Vol. 2 – Chapter 12

Six Tonic Major Triads, Alt. Asc. and Desc.

Six Tonic Major Triads, Alt. Desc and Asc.

Made in the USA
Lexington, KY
20 December 2014